NATIONAL GEOGRAPHIC

From Work to School

PATHFINDER EDITION

By Shirleyann Costigan

CONTENTS

From Work to School

By Shirleyann Costigan

Boys tend the machines in a cotton mill around 1910.

What does "work" mean to you?

Maybe it means doing a few chores such as cleaning your room, washing the dishes, taking out the trash. Maybe it means earning money to spend however you choose. Whatever work means to you, there are times when you wish you didn't have to do it. Adults may tell you that work is a necessary part of growing up; it builds helpful skills, it develops a sense of responsibility, and it teaches the true value of money. This is all very true, but no child wants to work all the time.

Yet children in America have always worked. Children worked on farms, in the fields, in shops, and in **factories** right alongside adults. The work was not always bad for them, but sometimes it was. Many children worked long hours for little or no **pay**. Sometimes, unhealthy conditions in the workplace made them sick. There is a name for this kind of work; it is called "child labor."

Laws in America **protect** children from being exploited, or taken advantage of for someone else's **profit**. Today, child labor laws limit the number of hours children can work. These laws also require **employers** to provide safe places and fair wages for child workers.

It may be difficult to believe, but such laws did not always exist in America. Where they did exist, they were often ignored.

In those days, childhood for America's children was very different than it is today.

A Changing America

At the beginning of 19th century, America was still a rural country; most people lived outside the big cities. Children who lived on farms or in small towns knew what it was to work. Some helped out in the fields. Most of them helped out with daily chores in the home. Town children often worked part-time in the family business. The children did not work for pay. They worked to contribute to their families' well being. Since a child's parents were the employers, no one saw the need for laws to protect child workers.

During the 19th century, machines began to replace hand labor in a process called industrialization. This process put many people out of work, so they migrated to larger towns and cities to find jobs. Some of the poorer families went to work in large factories. Their employers were the factory managers. The managers' job was to make as big a profit as possible. To increase profits, the managers needed cheap labor, and the cheapest laborers they could hire were women and children.

A young girl helps with the potato harvest.

Teens work with large machines in a mill.

Twelve-year-old Fursen Owens

Children at Work

Children from the ages of five to sixteen years old worked in many workplaces, but especially in factories. They might work twelve to eighteen hours, six days a week. For this much work they were paid a dollar—sometimes less. The youngest children usually worked alongside their mothers to earn a bit more money, so they were paid only pennies a day. Child workers didn't keep the money. Every penny they earned helped to support their families.

Some older children were given time off to attend school, but they were usually too tired to learn and had no time to study. Many children did not attend school at all. Twelve-year-old Fursen Owens had been working for four years. He couldn't read and didn't know his A,B,C's. "Yes, I want to learn," he said, "but I can't when I work all the time."

Working conditions in the factories were often unhealthy, so children became sick. Many died young. Working around big machines could be dangerous, too. Children were injured and even killed, but the work went on.

Factories were not the only places that employed children. Children also worked in coal mines, in the fishing industry, on street corners selling newspapers, or at home making paper flowers to sell in the streets. Children as young as three years old worked in their one-room apartments helping their mothers sew buttons on garments for clothing makers. Older brothers and sisters who attended school would return home and stitch clothing until late at night to earn a few more pennies for their family. Whatever work they did, children of poor families labored long hours for little pay. Their health and their education suffered.

Students stand outside a common school.

Two girls head off to school.

School and Play

When America was still largely a nation of family farms, children rarely completed high school. In rural areas, children often went to school only when they were not working in the fields. The schools they attended were called common schools. Parent donations or state taxes paid for the common schools. Children from six to sixteen studied in the same room and were taught by the same teacher. Students had no books, no pencils or paper—only a slate and piece of chalk.

In the 1800s, there was never much time for play. When not in school, children either worked full-time or helped out at home. Chores, from baking bread to pumping water from the well, had to be done everyday. Toys were simple, handmade, and passed down to each new sister or brother. Books were rare, and they were read by candlelight.

Wordwise

employer: person or company that you work for

factory: large building where people use machines to make goods

pay: money that your employer gives you for work you have done

profit: amount of money you get when you sell something for more than it cost

protect: to keep someone or something safe from harm or damage

Public Schools and Parks

By the early 1900s, America was transformed. New inventions, such as the telephone and electric lights, made life easier. Family life had changed, too, as more families worked and lived the cities.

At the same time, attitudes toward children were changing. Church leaders and concerned citizens began to object to children's working conditions. They recognized that working children received little or no education. People began to realize that education would make children better citizens and better workers. So it was clear to them that all children, even the very poor, needed to work less and go to school more. This was a very new idea.

Public schools, run by the state, replaced the small common schools. In public schools, students were separated by their ages into grades. Each grade had its own classroom. More books were available, but most students still used a slate and chalk. The school year was extended to six or even nine months. Discipline was very strict. Children didn't dare fool around in school.

School time had never been playtime, but an increasing number of public parks and city playgrounds made real playtime more accessible. Manufactured toys, such as model trains, teddy bears, Lincoln Logs, crayons, and bikes, became very popular.

Public organizations were looking out for children, too. The Young Men's Christian Association (YMCA) opened gyms and gave free swimming lessons to boys. Later, it began to admit girls into its organization. The Boy Scouts of America opened its first office in 1910. Other scout groups for both boys and girls soon followed. The purpose of these organizations was to help young people become healthy, caring adults.

Finally, in 1938, the U.S. Congress passed fair labor laws nationwide. The laws limited the number of hours a child could work. They also required employers to pay children at least twenty-five cents an hour. (In those days, twenty-five cents would buy two movie tickets and a box of popcorn.) To keep children out of dangerous workplaces, the laws limited the kinds of jobs a child could have. Soon, fewer children were working full-time and more were attending school. By that time, all children from ages eight to fourteen were required to attend school. These laws are still in effect today.

Boys play a game with marbles in the 1920s.

From Work to School
AROUND THE WORLD

Unbelievably, over 200 million children around the world still work long hours under unhealthy conditions. More than 90 million are under twelve years old. Now here's the good news. These numbers are not as high as they used to be. The numbers continue to go down because organizations, caring individuals, and children like you are making a difference.

"The bravest voice can live in the smallest body." That's what twelve-year-old Craig Kielburger learned when he read about Iqbal Masih. Twelve-year-old Iqbal was born in South Asia. He began to work with other children in a carpet factory at the age of four. He spent six years weaving carpets for a cruel employer. After he stopped working there, Iqbal was killed for speaking publicly against child labor.

Craig was so disturbed by this story that he decided to help children like Iqbal. He organized a group of his classmates. They signed petitions and faxed them to world leaders to complain about child labor. The kids raised money by organizing garage sales, car washes, and bake sales. They asked people for donations. They raised enough money to provide shelters and schools to keep children out of the factories. Craig named his organization Free the Children.

Today, Free the Children has helped to open more than 100 schools and recovery centers for child workers around the world.

Its goal is to see all children gain their basic human rights and freedoms. It is the world's largest network of children helping children.

Education is the key to a better life. Children who are educated grow up to become leaders, teachers, good citizens, and better parents. It is education for all children everywhere that will put an end to child labor.

Craig Kielburger with a student

The Photographs That

One man fights for justice with pictures.

Lewis Hine was a New York City schoolteacher and photographer. In the early 1900s, Hine took photographs of working children all over the United States. He exhibited his photographs and gave talks about the lives of working children. His words and pictures shocked the nation. More people began to speak out for child workers. His photographs helped to establish stronger child labor laws.

Lewis Hine took this picture of eight-year-old Michael McNelis. The boy was found selling newspapers during a rainstorm, although he had just recovered from a second attack of pneumonia. Newsboys made about thirty cents a day.

The "newsies," as they were called, were usually homeless and desperately poor, but they were a spunky lot. In 1899, thousands of newsboys went on strike to demand more money. One of the strikers, called Kid Blink because he was blind in one eye, made this speech to the crowd.

"Friens and feller workers. Dis is a time which tries de hearts of men. Dis is de time when we'se got to stick together like glue.... We know wot we wants and we'll git it even if we is blind."

–"NEWSIE" KID BLINK

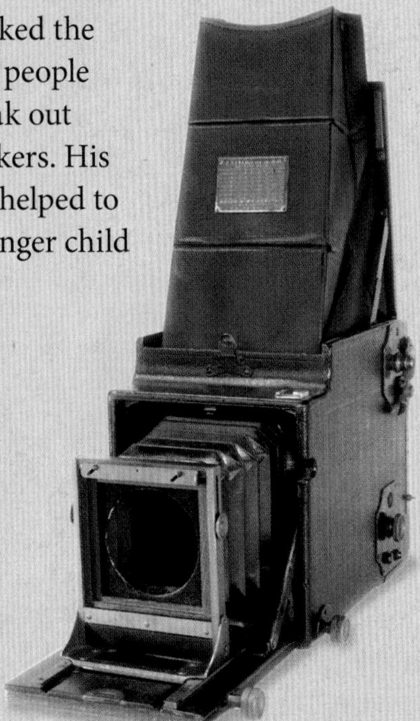

Changed the Nation

She was fifty-one inches high and had been working in the mill for one year. Sometimes she worked at night. She managed four machines for forty-eight cents a day.

When Lewis Hine asked this mill worker how old she was, she hesitated. Then she said, "I don't remember." But she added confidentially, "I'm not old enough to work, but do just the same."

Children and parents often lied about a child's age to get a job. Poor families needed the extra money, so everyone in the household had to work. There were laws that limited the number of hours a child could work, but children under ten years old often worked twelve hours a day.

The seafood industry employed all but the youngest babies in a family. Work could begin at 3:30 in the morning and end at 5:00 in the evening. Children used sharp knives to shuck, or cut, oysters from their shells and to chop fish. Slippery floors and benches and bumping into other workers increased the danger of accidents. "The salt water gets into the cuts and they ache," said one boy. It was a smelly job, too.

School Rules!

Answer these question about children moving from work to school.

1. List two ways that life changed from the 19th to the 20th century.

2. What kinds of work did children do on farms? How did work for children change when they started to work in factories?

3. How were common schools different from public schools?

4. How did the labor laws of 1938 help protect child workers?

5. How are the author's viewpoints about Iqbal on page 8 and the "newsies" on page 10 similar? How do the viewpoints differ?